VOCAL/PIANO SOLO

DAVID LANZ   KRISTIN AMARIE

SILHOUETTES OF LOVE

Cover design by Kristin Amarie Lanz
Artist photo by Jeff Fasano
Editing by Kathy Parsons
Original *Silhouettes of Love* album available at
Davidlanz.com
Amariemusic.com

ISBN 978-1-4950-9820-8

HAL•LEONARD®
7777 W. BLUEMOUND RD. P.O. BOX 13819 MILWAUKEE, WI 53213

In Australia Contact:
Hal Leonard Australia Pty. Ltd.
4 Lentara Court
Cheltenham, Victoria, 3192 Australia
Email: ausadmin@halleonard.com.au

Visit Hal Leonard Online at
www.halleonard.com

THE SOARING HEART

Music and Lyrics by DAVID LANZ
and KRISTIN AMARIE LANZ

(R.H. over L.H.)

mf

THE PROMISE

Music and Lyrics by DAVID LANZ
and KRISTIN AMARIE LANZ

Moderately, expressively

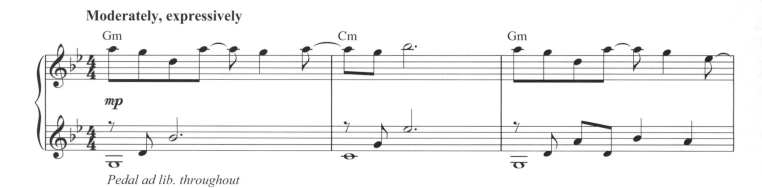

Pedal ad lib. throughout

The heart speaks in

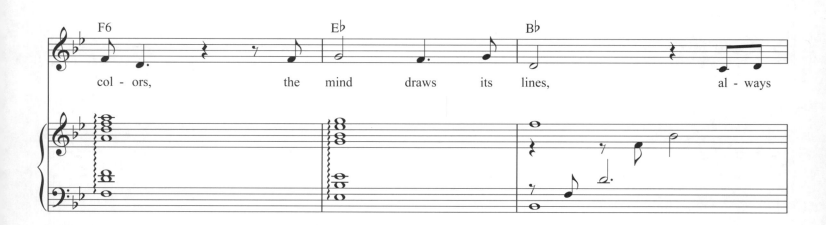

col- ors,   the mind draws its lines,   al - ways

look - ing _____ for an - swers, pray - ing al - ways to

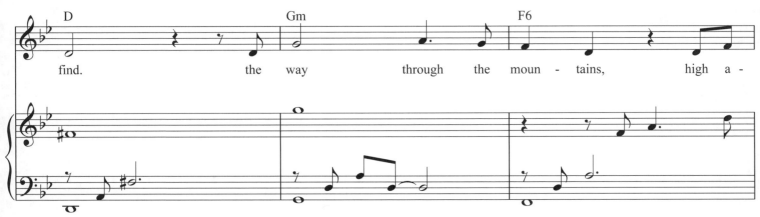

find. the way through the moun - tains, high a -

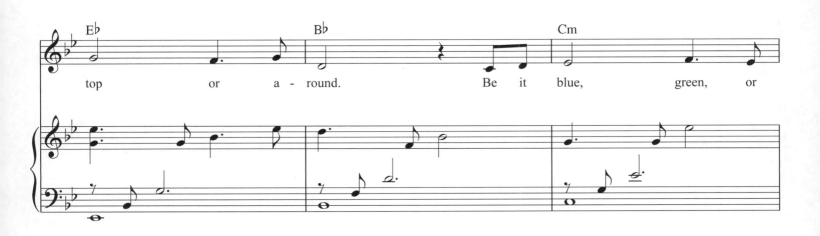

top or a - round. Be it blue, green, or

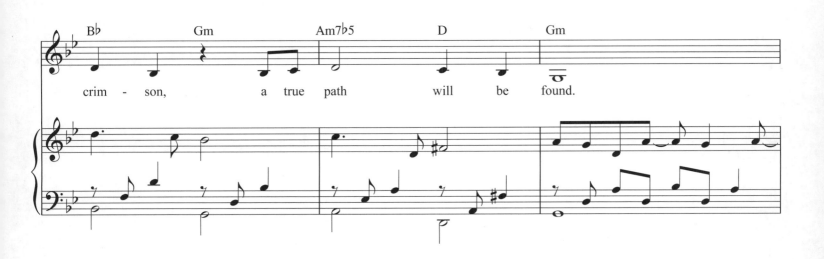

crim - son, a true path will be found.

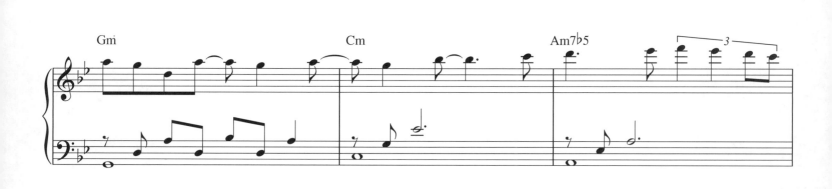

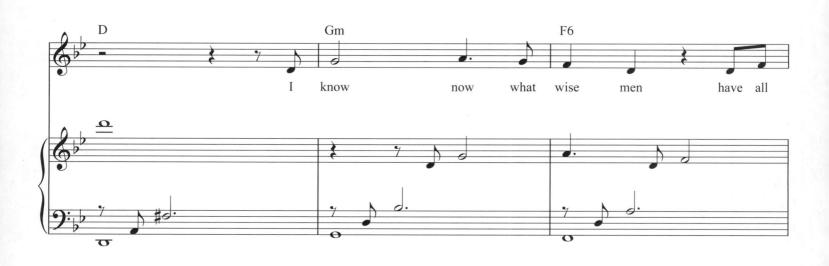

I know now what wise men have all

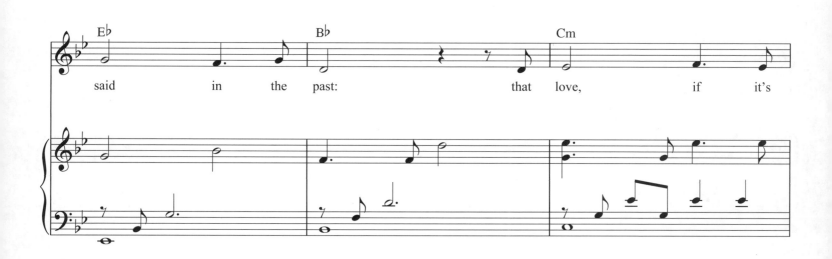

said in the past: that love, if it's

er to me. _____

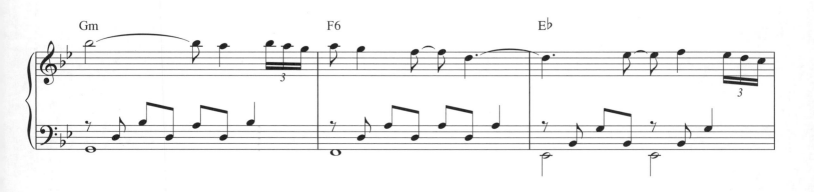

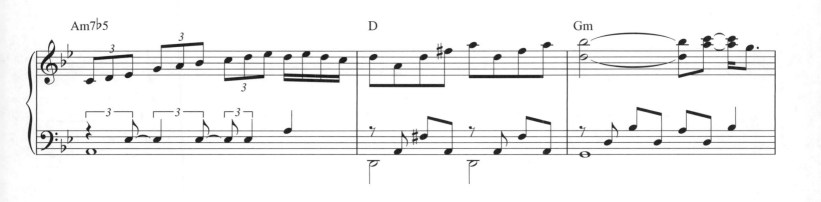

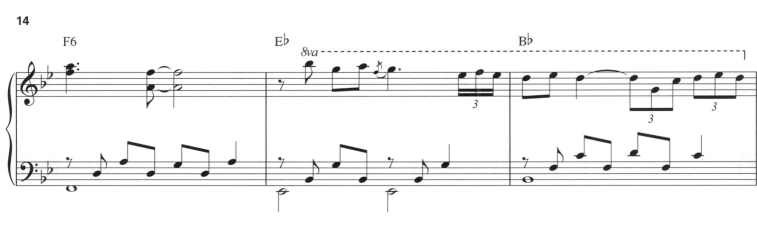

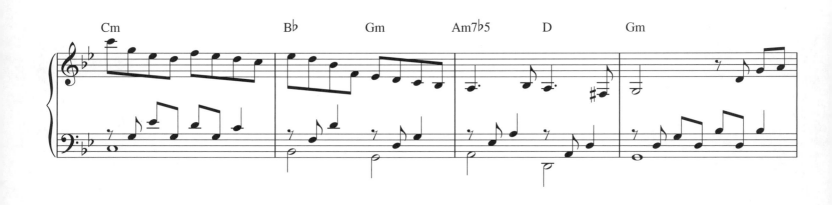

The heart _____ sings in rain - bows _____

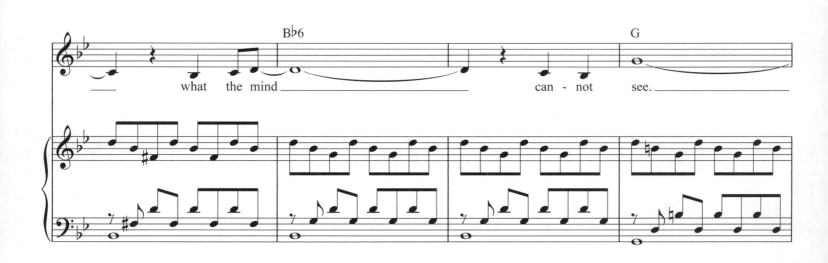

_____ what the mind _____ can - not see.

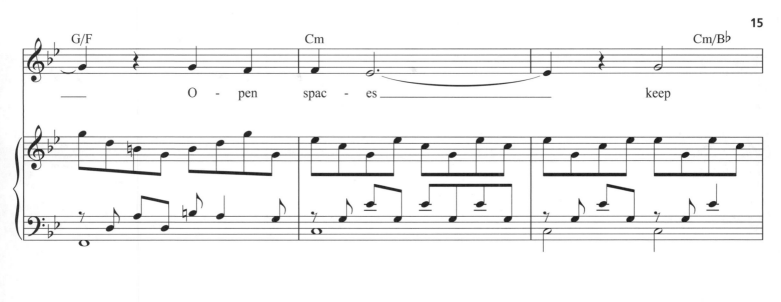

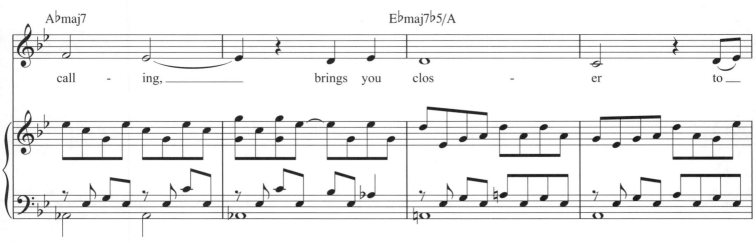

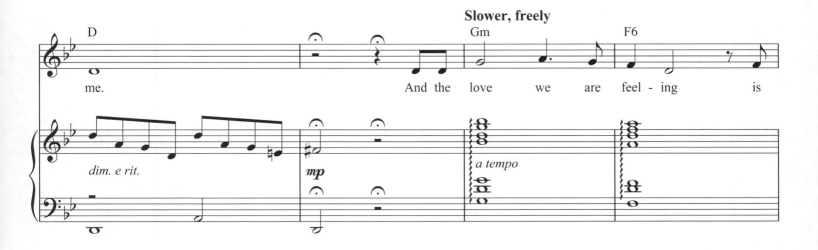

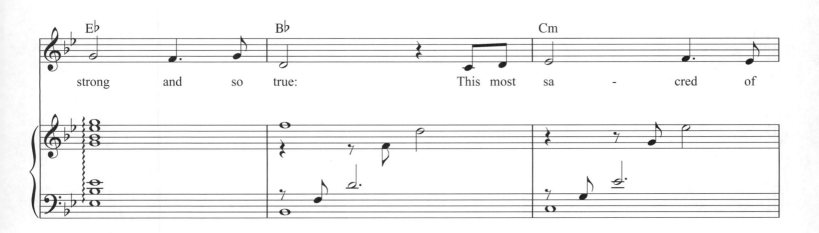

CIRCLES ROUND THE MOON

Music and Lyrics by DAVID LANZ
and KRISTIN AMARIE LANZ

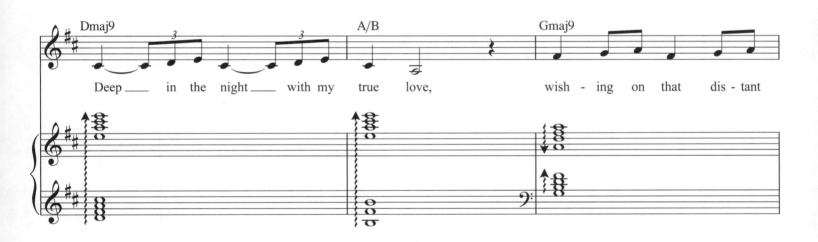

Deep ___ in the night ___ with my true love, wish - ing on that dis - tant

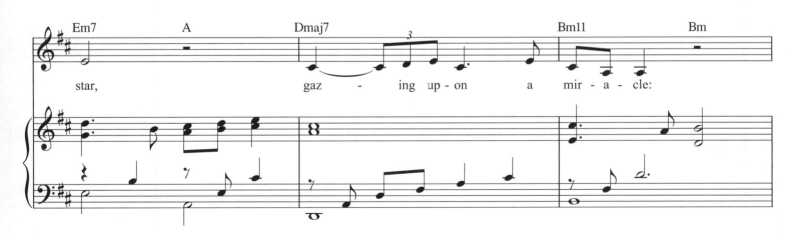

star, gaz - ing up - on a mir - a - cle:

Lyrics:
wish - ing on that dis - tant star, gaz - ing up - on a
mir - a - cle: heav - en-ly light _____ from a - far. _____

Freely

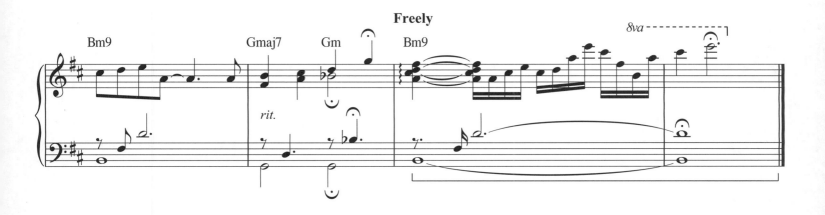

FALLING

Music and Lyrics by DAVID LANZ
and KRISTIN AMARIE LANZ

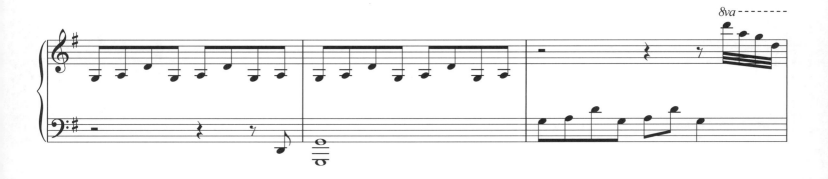

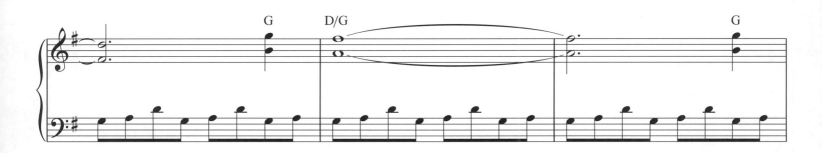

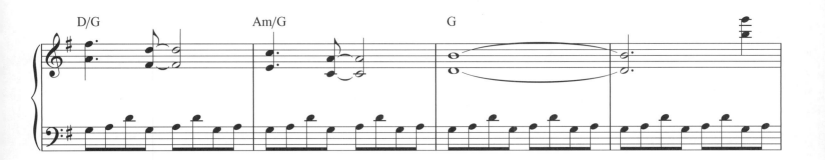

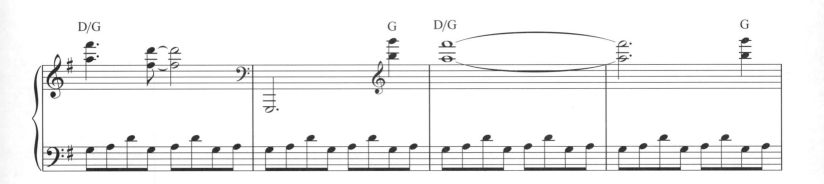

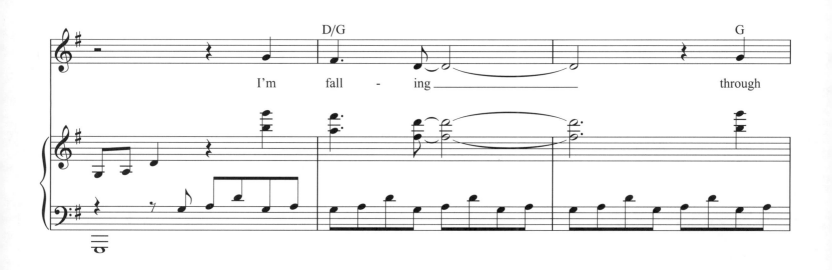

I'm fall - ing _____ through _____ time.

I'm search - ing _____ for

signs. _____

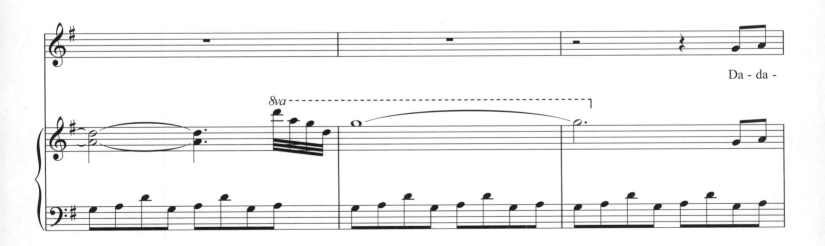

Da - da -

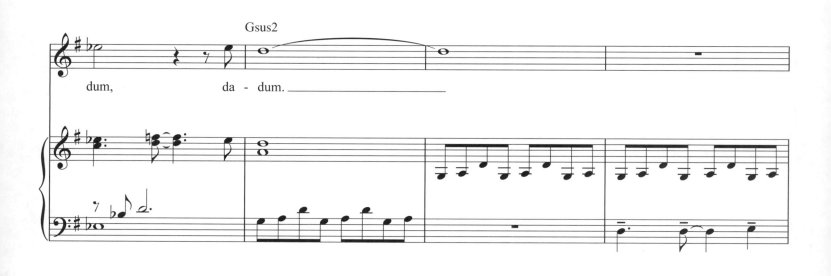

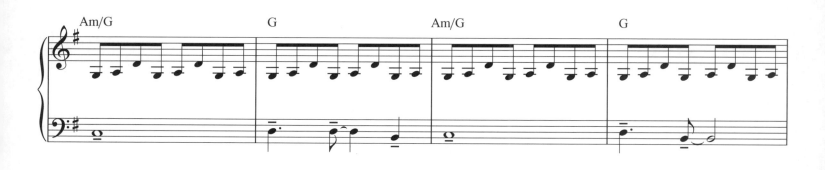

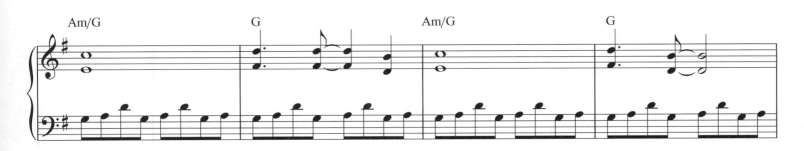

Da-da-dum - da - dum -

da, da-da-dum - da - da-da, ba-

da. _____ Still

FOUND BY LOVE'S RETURN

Music and Lyrics by DAVID LANZ
and KRISTIN AMARIE LANZ

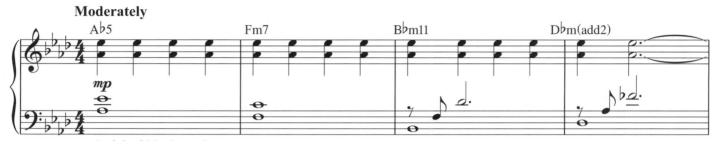

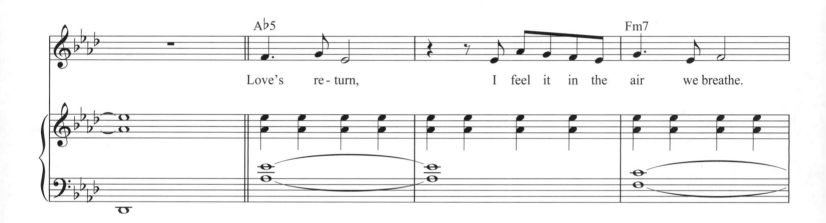

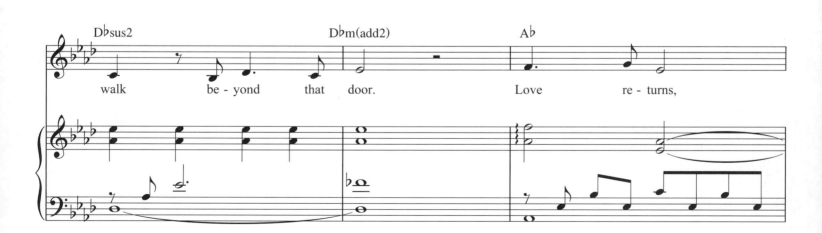

we o-pen up our hearts to-night, let-ting go of

all our fear, reach-ing out to touch the one who

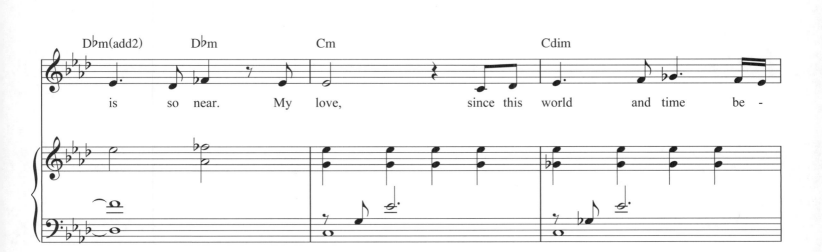

is so near. My love, since this world and time be-

gan, you and I've walked hand in hand; and this

love will go on and on ___ and on ___

and on. ___ I see you in the

stars, I feel you in the wind, I hear you in a song ___

that nev-er stops ___ and nev-er fades. ___ And when the night has

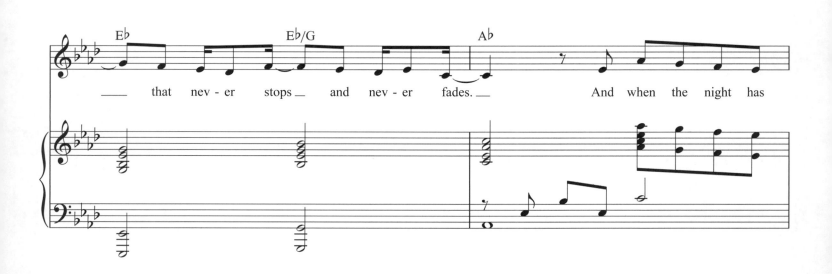

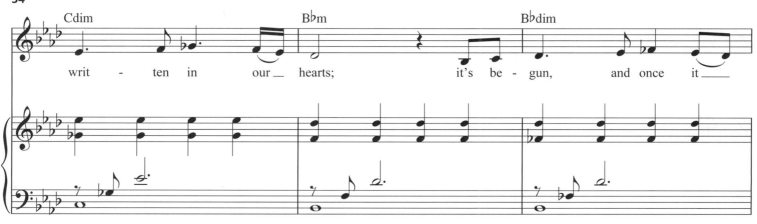

writ - ten in our __ hearts; it's be - gun, and once it __

starts then this song will play on and on __ and on __

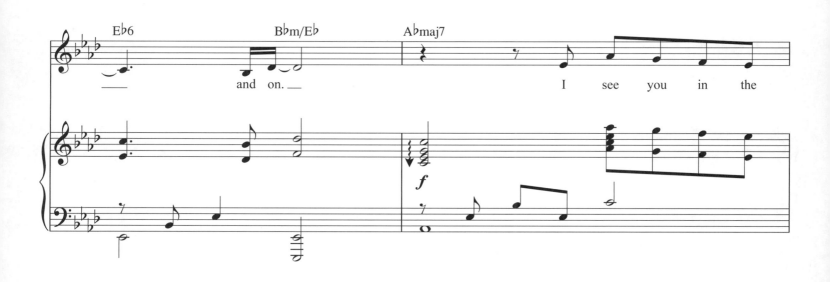

__ and on. __ I see you in the

stars, I feel you in the wind, I hear you in a song __

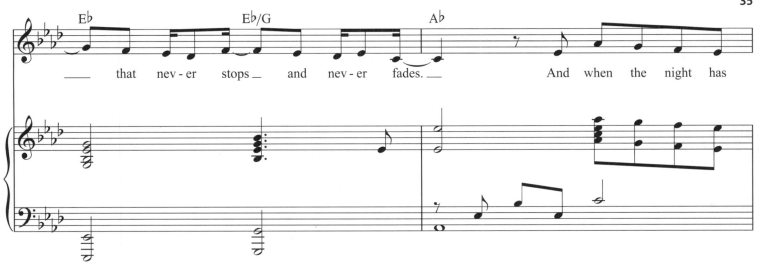

that nev-er stops ___ and nev-er fades. ___ And when the night has

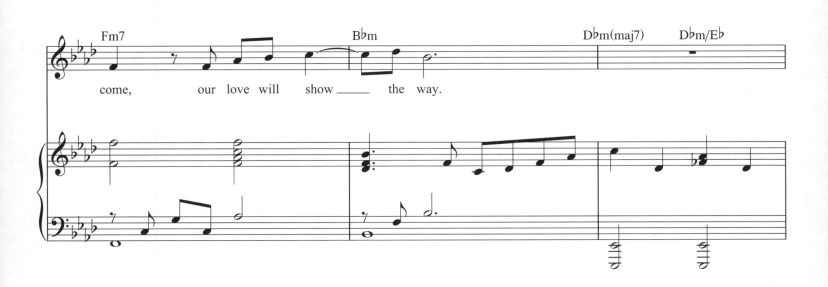

come, ___ our love will show ___ the way.

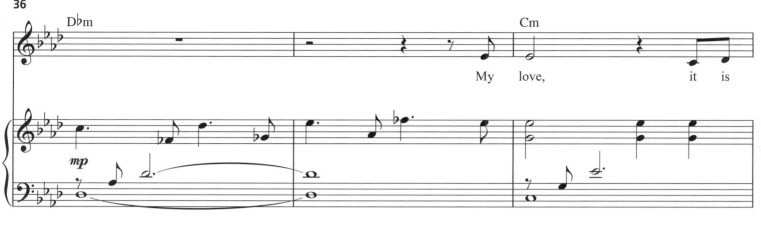

My love, it is

writ - ten in our __ hearts; it's be - gun, and once it __

starts, then this song will play on and on __ and on __

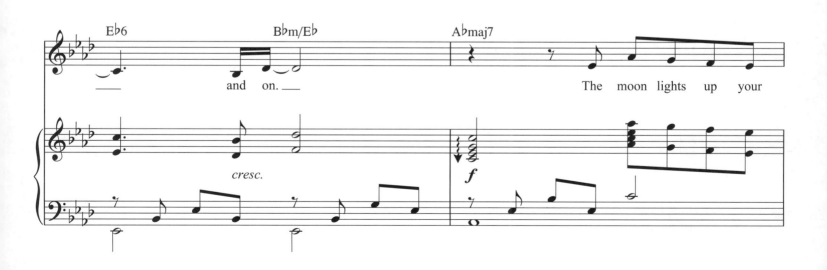

__ and on. __ The moon lights up your

LADY ON THE SHORE

Music and Lyrics by DAVID LANZ
and KRISTIN AMARIE LANZ

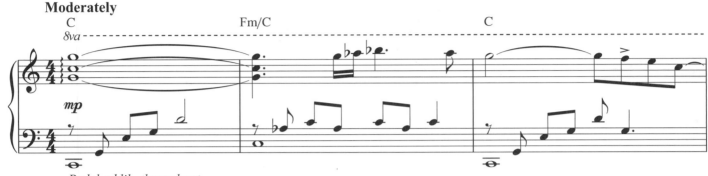

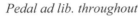

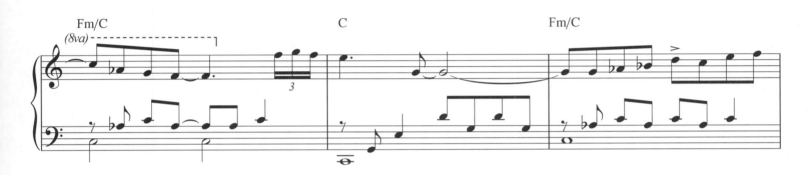

My life _____ be - gan a - new when first my eyes saw you; a rose with - in my soul a-

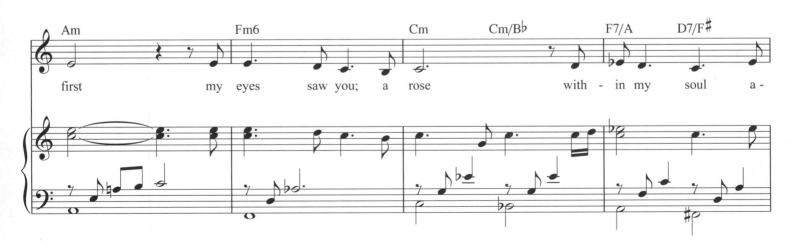

shore. I'm the one _____ you've wait-ed for. A-bove the

waves I will rise. on your tide. _____

The one you've wait - ed for. I'm your

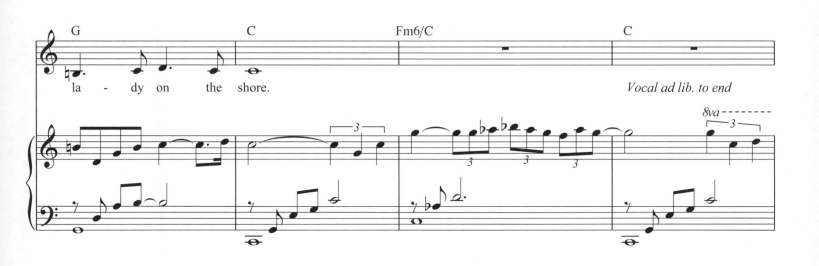

la - dy on the shore.

Vocal ad lib. to end

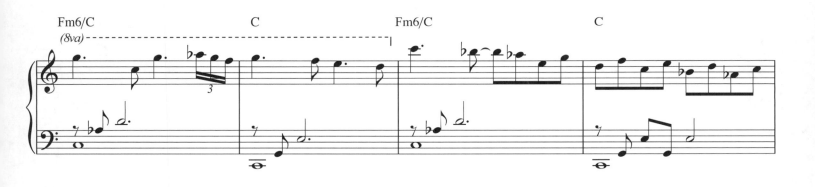

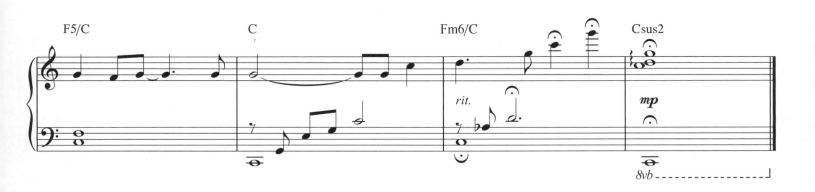

rit.

mp

SILHOUETTE OF LOVE

Music and Lyrics by DAVID LANZ
and KRISTIN AMARIE LANZ

Moderately

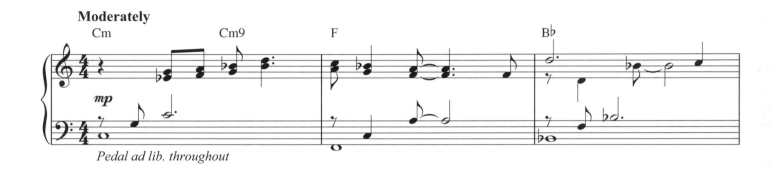

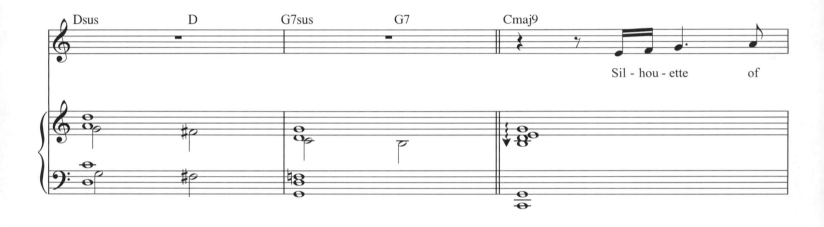

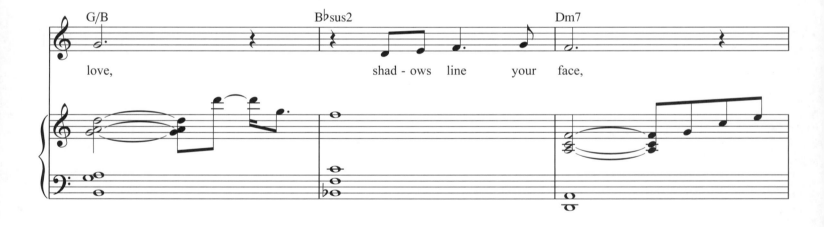

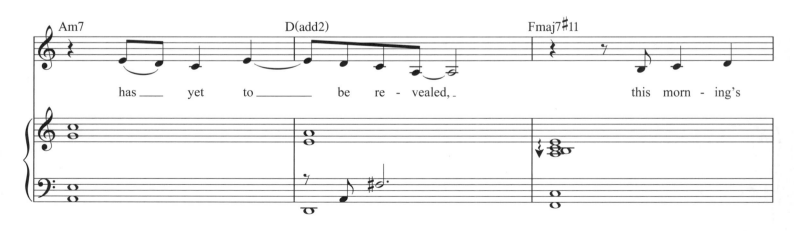

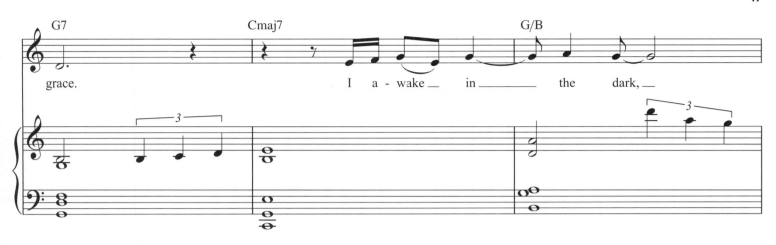

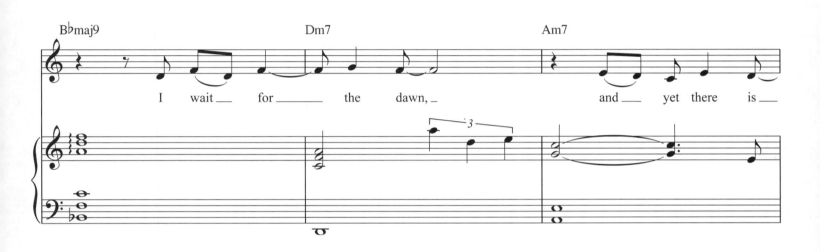

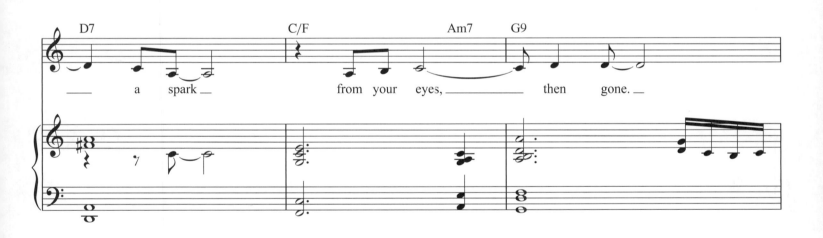

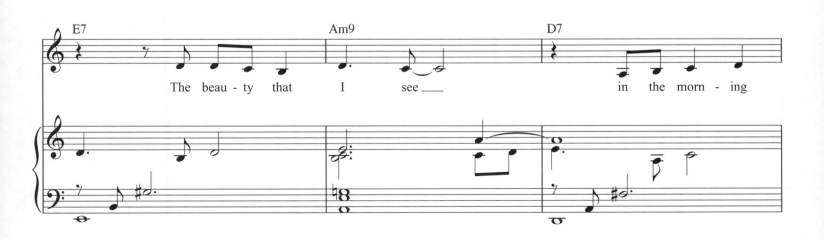

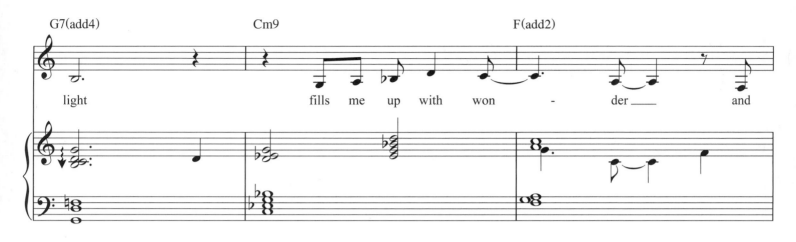

light   fills me up with won - der _____ and

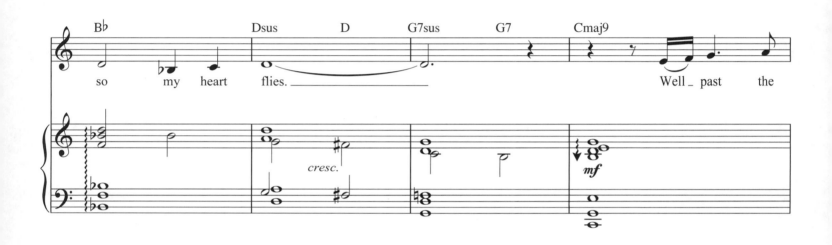

so   my heart flies. _____ Well _ past the

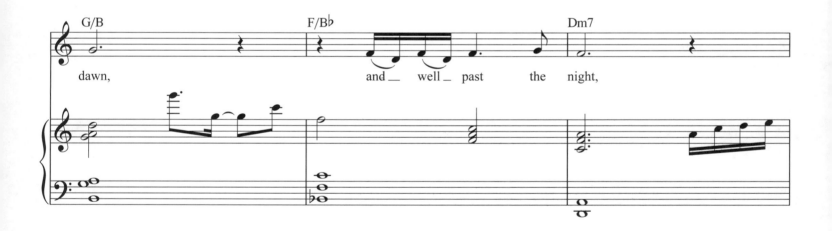

dawn,   and _ well _ past the night,

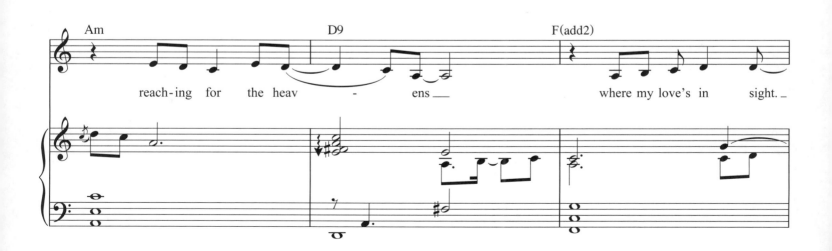

reach-ing for the heav - ens ___ where my love's in sight. _

The beau-ty that I _____ see

in the morn - ing light _____ fills me up with won -

- der, _____ and so my heart flies. _____

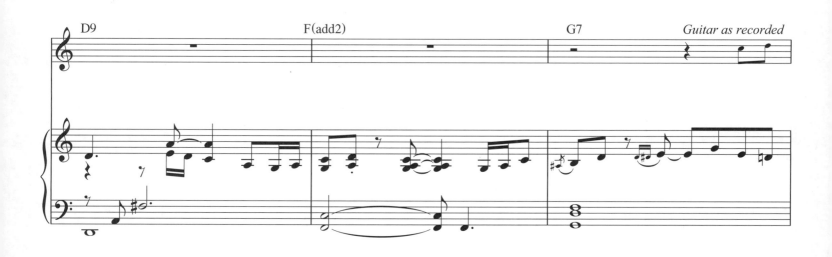

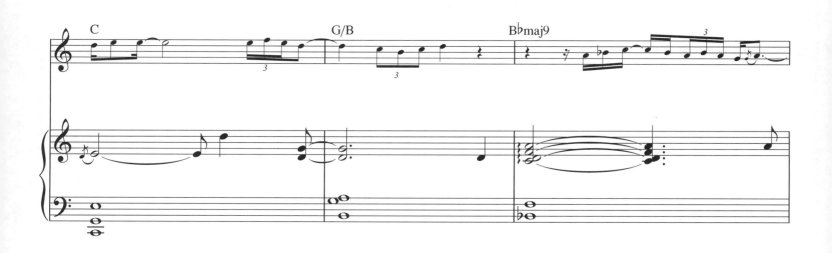

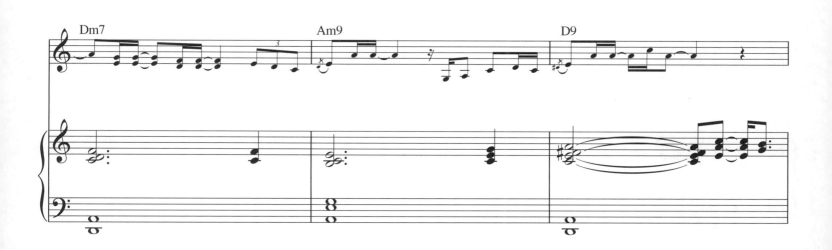

The beau - ty that I ____ ____ see in the morn - ing light, sil - hou - ette ____ of ____ true love, _____ makes my heart __ fly. _____

OUR ILLUSION

Music and Lyrics by DAVID LANZ
and KRISTIN AMARIE LANZ

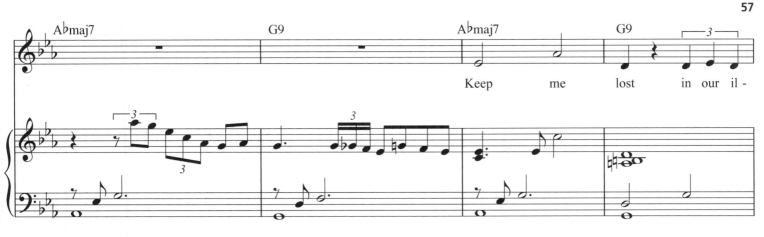

Keep me lost in our il -

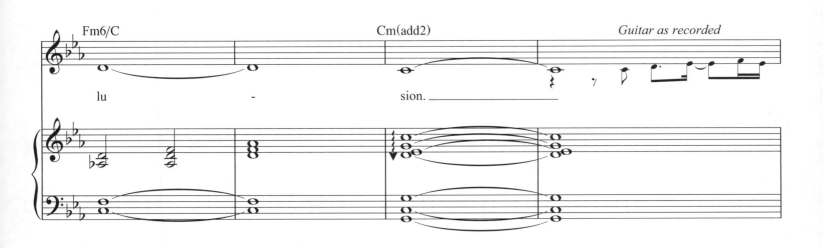

lu - sion.

Guitar as recorded

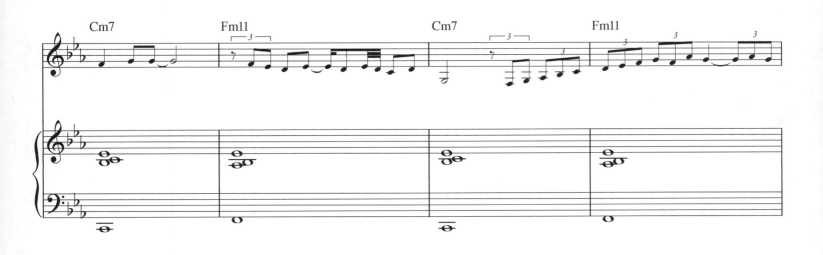

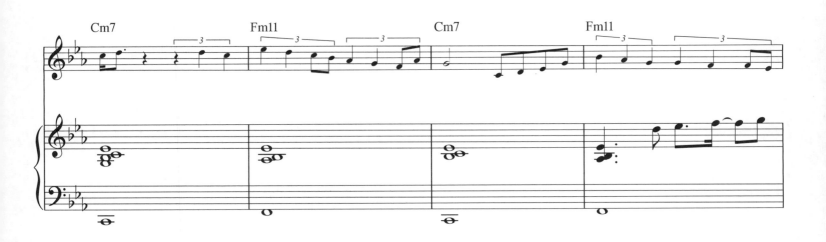

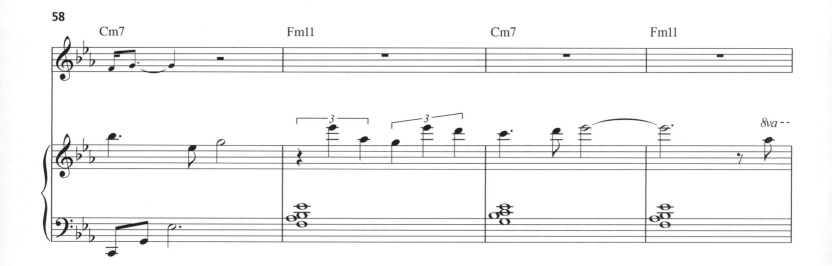

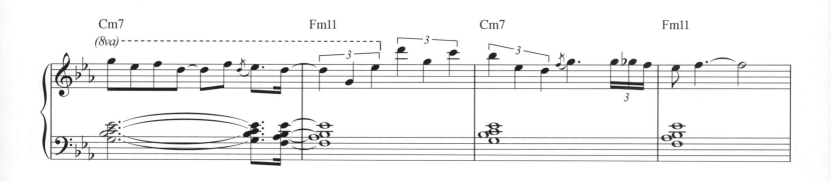

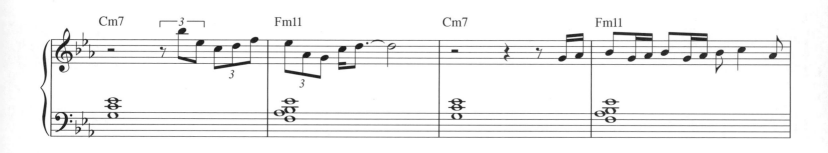

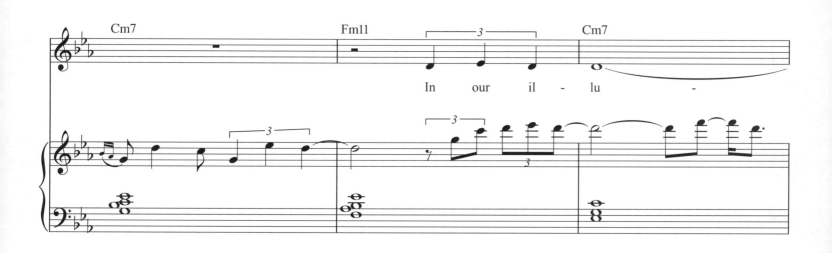

In our il - lu -

AMORE ETERNO REDUX

Music by KRISTIN AMARIE LANZ

L.H.: Synthesizer arranged for piano

R.H.: Piano as recorded

L.H.: Piano and ensemble arranged for piano

R.H.: Guitar arranged for piano

Both hands: Piano as recorded

Both hands: Ensemble arranged for piano

Both hands: Piano as recorded

DANTE AND BEATRICE
(Fra Beatrice)

Music and Lyrics by
KRISTIN AMARIE LANZ

Moderately, flowing, in 2

Pedal ad lib. throughout

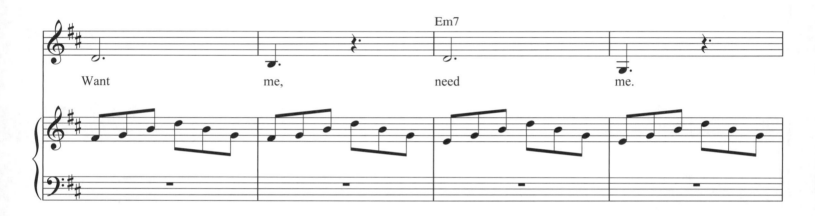

Want me, need me.

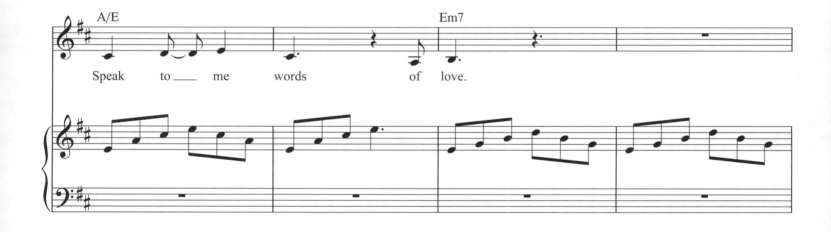

Speak to ___ me words of love.

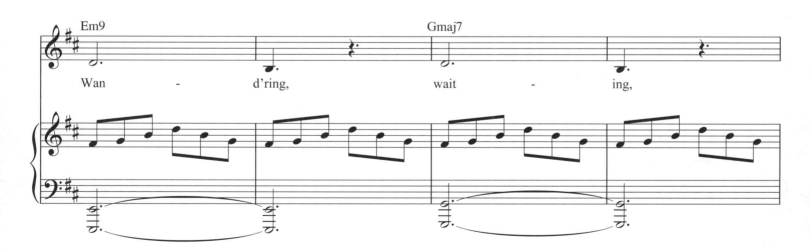

Wan - d'ring, wait - ing,

WAITING FOR THE SUN

Music and Lyrics by DAVID LANZ
and KRISTIN AMARIE LANZ

Moderately

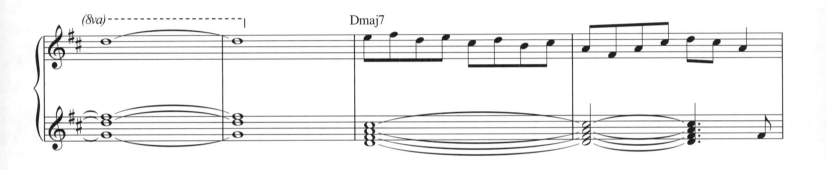

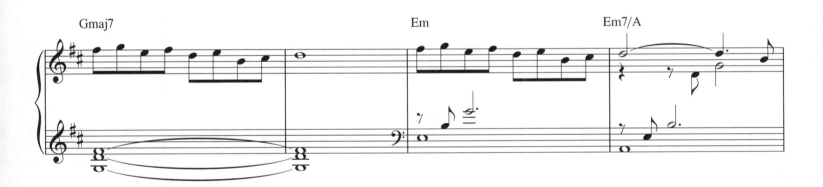

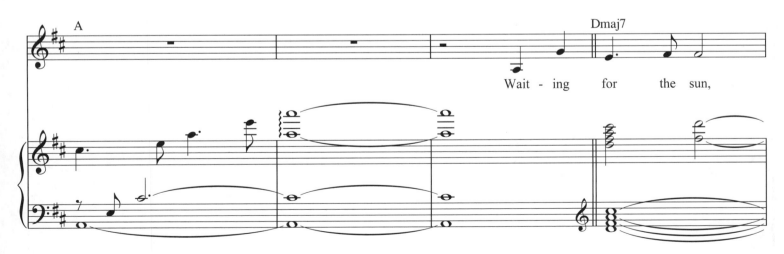

Wait-ing for the sun,

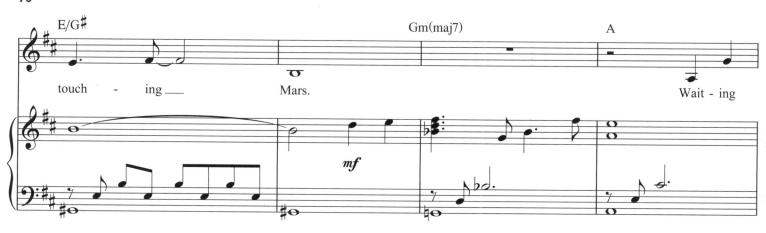

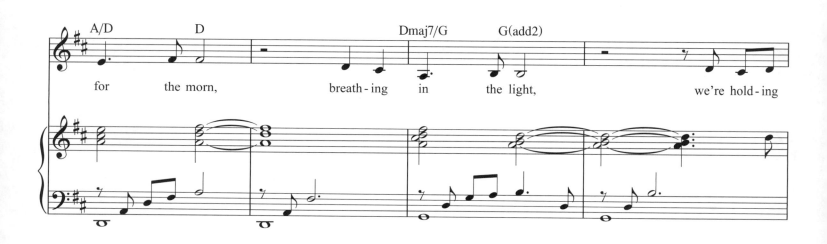

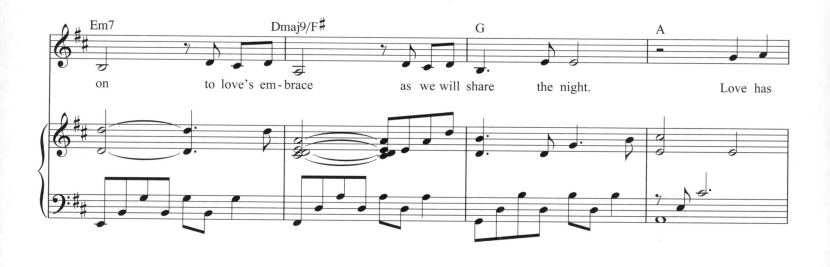

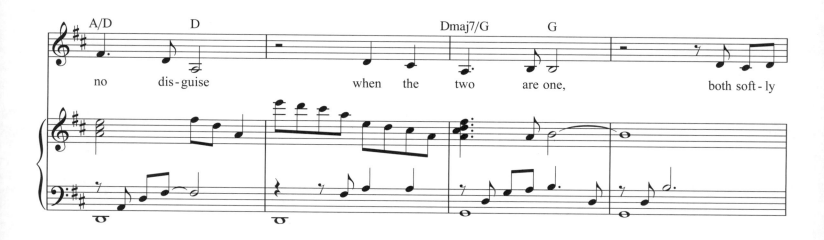

SO IN LOVE

Music and Lyrics by DAVID LANZ
and KRISTIN AMARIE LANZ

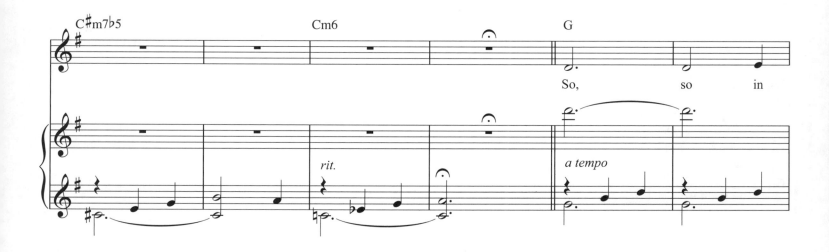

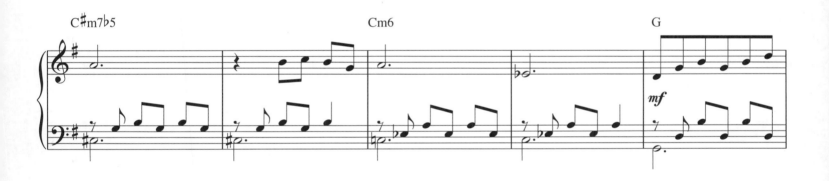

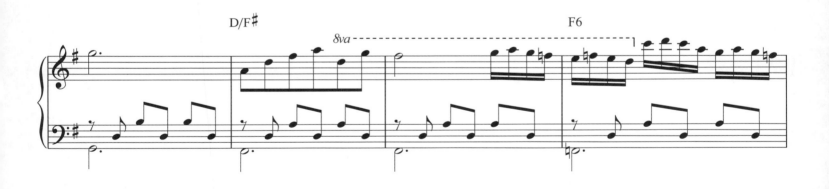

SILVER THREADS
(Without You)

Music and Lyrics by DAVID LANZ
and KRISTIN AMARIE LANZ

Hear my voice, it's reach - ing out in

sil - ver threads for you.